Martha's Vineyard and Nantucket

Martha's Vineyard and Nantucket

Author

Bill Harris

Photography

Tom Kelly and Gail Mooney

CLB 2578
© 1991 Colour Library Books Ltd, Godalming, Surrey, England.
All rights reserved.
This 1991 edition published by Crescent Books,
distributed by Outlet Book Company, Inc, a Random House Company,
225 Park Avenue South, New York, New York 10003.
Color reproduction by Scantrans Pte Ltd, Singapore.
Printed and bound in Hong Kong.
ISBN 0 517 05310 1
8 7 6 5 4 3 2 1

CRESCENT BOOKS
NEW YORK

Tranquil Great Pond, Martha's Vineyard.

Which is better, Martha's Vineyard or Nantucket?

Asking such a question on either island will get you a lively argument, more often than not from someone who's never actually been to the other one, even though it is only twenty miles across the water, but is absolutely positive there couldn't possibly be another place anywhere quite as charming as the Vineyard....or Nantucket. There are differences, of course. Nantucket is about half the size of Martha's Vineyard, and is further out at sea. But there are as many similarities as differences, even though they are usually only apparent to the people the natives insist on calling the "off-islanders."

The first of those off-islanders was Captain Bartholomew Gosnold who explored Nantucket Sound and Vineyard Sound in 1602. He and his men wrote glowing accounts of the islands off the coast of Cape Cod, but the one Gosnold called Martha's Vineyard (some say to honor his daughter, others insist it was his mother-in-law) was probably one of the sixteen Elizabeth Islands a few miles off the present day Vineyard's north shore at the edge of Buzzard's Bay. He apparently intended to stay because he built a house on Cuttyhunk, the southernmost island in the chain, but his homesick crew talked him into setting sail for England.

Signposts of welcome and warning. Some of Chilmark's roads are private.

Is a cycle an "unauthorized vehicle?" These youngsters may soon find out.

He went back to America four years later as part of a colonizing party sent out by the Virginia Company. They landed at the entrance to Chesapeake Bay, and in spite of Gosnold's protests that they should be thinking of settling further north, they established their colony at Jamestown. More than half of them, including Gosnold, were dead of malaria and fever within six months. It is not recorded whether Gosnold's last words were "I told you so."

The first Englishmen who saw Martha's Vineyard, like visitors who will see it for the first time next summer, obviously fell in love with the place. They were impressed by the fishing, which they said was much better than in the Grand Banks off Newfoundland. Further north, they pointed out, the fish were in waters five times deeper and much further off shore. They found the coastline "as free from dangers as any" and the land itself as perfect as any man could hope to see. Beech and cedar trees and tall oaks were plentiful, wild peas grew everywhere they looked; the strawberries were much bigger and sweeter than any they had ever seen, and there were fruit-producing vines all over the place, "where we could not go for treading upon them." An experimental planting produced healthy crops of wheat, barley and oats with almost no effort. They found the island rich in deer and fowl, too, and great freshwater ponds and springs abounded in all parts of the island. They also noted that there was an abundance of stones for building, and finally concluded that, in comparison, "England is but barren."

If such information were included in a real estate prospectus, the Vineyard would probably have been sold before the ink was dry. But it wasn't until 1641 that the English noblemen who had a claim to the islands finally found a buyer when Thomas Mayhew of the Bay Colony bought Martha's Vineyard, the Elizabeth Islands and Nantucket from them for forty pounds.

Another year passed before his son and namesake went out to have a look at the new family holdings and decided to stay. Along with other investors, he established a new town

The gray of weathered cedar shingles is common in Edgartown, where the colors of flowers are complemented by the family wash (above) on a blue Monday morning.

Edgartown, the Vineyard's first settlement, became the island's most affluent after whaling captains built grand, white clapboard houses in the nineteenth century.

they decided to call Great Harbor. The harbor is, indeed, great, but the settlement eventually became known as Old Town and finally Edgartown. But the harbor wasn't what interested them. In the spring millions of herring went up the nearby creeks to spawn in the freshwater ponds. Over time, the industrious Vineyarders were harvesting three quarters of a million of the fish in an average year and were banking thousands of dollars in an era when a family could live comfortably on less than two hundred.

The island was created when a great glacier came to rest and dumped sand and boulders in a triangular pattern in the sea as it was carving out Cape Cod. But, like the Cape, it is constantly being re-created by the action of the sea. Prevailing southwest winds push the surf against the Vineyard shore at a sharp angle and the sand is constantly moving from west to east, opening new channels and closing old ones unpredictably. Finally, the men who had claimed a monopoly on the herring business solved the problem by digging a canal between the sea and the Great Pond, and the industry continued until the late 19th century, when the world seems to have lost its taste for herring.

But long before then, men who were deriding the herring monopolists by calling their catch Old Town turkeys had found a much more lucrative creature in the sea. In the early 18th century, John Coffin, a relative newcomer to the Vineyard, began sending small ships to trade at the Southern ports and Cuba and eventually dispatched them around the tip of South America to gather the treasures of the Orient. But before long, his ships and those of other

Edgartown harbor in high summer.

Above: scarlet geraniums in a window box enhance a view of Edgartown harbor.

Dusk falls over Edgartown harbor.

Above: waiting for the mail at West Chop.

At Vineyard Haven, you can recover from the night before with a little hair of the dog at the Black Dog Tavern (facing page).

enterprising Vineyarders rounded the horn in search of whales.

Nantucket was the undisputed center of the whaling business at the time, but Martha's Vineyard was her partner. The fully loaded whaling ships had difficulty crossing the bar at the entrance to Nantucket's harbor, and it was customary to put in to Edgartown for a final fitting-out before going to sea and to call there again on the way back to lighten their load before going home. And to the masters of many of the ships, Edgartown was home. Vineyard captains commanded ships based in New Bedford, too, and some even operated from Sag Harbor on Long Island. If the Vineyard's own fleet was

small, the profits from other ports helped make Edgartown a showplace of impressive mansions and churches.

At the same time, Vineyard Haven was bringing wealth to the island aboard coastal trading vessels passing through Vineyard Sound. More than a thousand vessels a week passed the island in the 1830s and many of them put in at what was known as Holmes Hole in those days to ride out storms, to wait for the tide or catch a fresh wind. They used the stopovers as an opportunity to take on fresh supplies or to have local artisans repair damage, and the locals knew an opportunity when they saw one. Few harbors on the coast were better suited

as a port in a storm. And few are easier to find. It is protected by two high headlands called West Chop and East Chop because of their resemblance to the jaws of a vise.

The Vineyard Haven boom ended in 1914 when the Cape Cod Canal began taking coastal traffic away from the Sound, but by then the Vineyard had discovered a whole new industry by looking inward from the sea. In 1872, a pair of sea captains bought a huge portion of West Chop for four hundred dollars and sold it before the summer ended for ten thousand. And that was before fresh water was pumped up from Tashmoo springs to make it habitable. Once it had running water, West Chop became a self-contained, very restricted colony for well-heeled Bostonians who maintained their own beach, tennis courts, parks, cottages, a casino and an almost fanatical desire to be left alone.

But by the time society arrived, the East Chop headland had been attracting the hoi polloi for more than fifty years. And if they lacked mammon, they more than made up for it in Godliness. In 1835, a preacher named Jeremiah Pease set out from Edgartown in search of a place to praise God in a setting properly removed from the taint of worldliness. He found the spot a little more than seven miles away in a grove of oak trees overlooking a pond that would later become Oak Bluffs harbor. Rather than searching the Scriptures for an appropriate name, he called it Wesleyan Grove in honor of the founder of the Methodist Church. By mid-August, he had established a little tent community and was preaching from behind a lectern he had made himself from driftwood.

A couple sail their all-white yacht around Menemsha Pond.

Beauties in black at Dukes County Horse Show.

Within a few summers, his revivals were among the most popular in New England and the faithful arrived by the boatload to spent their brief vacations in the cool grove inhaling the tangy salt air and bathing their souls in the word of God. At first they were quartered in so-called "society tents," each with a curtain in the center to keep the men and women separate from one another. The tents weren't the last word in comfort – the faithful slept on the ground which was strewn with straw – but comfort wasn't what they came to find. In a few years,

though, the preacher responded to the demands of some of his followers to be able to separate themselves from the common herd and established a circle of family tents that offered an opportunity for them "to be more domestic in their household affairs." It was only a matter of time before domesticity became as desirable as purity of spirit, and in 1859, a Rhode Islander arrived at Wesleyan Grove with a prefabricated, Victorian-style cottage. Before long, local contractors were obliging other campers with jigsawed crockets and finials and Gothic arched doors and windows that the revival fans found acceptable because they thought the Victorian details made the

tents resemble churches. Eventually, of course, the tents were replaced by proper cottages and people began staying even after the revival meetings were over for the season.

Though it wasn't what he had in mind, Pease had created the Vineyard's first summer colony. Then, in 1868, some enterprising locals began speculating in land surrounding the original grove. They built a hotel and developed homesites and parks. They also introduced such worldly pleasures as a skating rink, but in deference to the neighbors, skaters waltzed to revivalist hymns rather than the sinful rhythms of the decadent Viennese. But that wasn't good enough for the church

people, who separated themselves from the Oak Bluffs development with a seven-foot picket fence.

In spite of his legacy to the land speculators, Pease would much rather be remembered for the number of souls he had wrested from the ranks of the Congregationalists and steered into the paths of Methodism. He had held his revival meetings in a huge tent, but in 1870 his successors were affluent enough to build an elegant, iron-arched Tabernacle that was one of the architectural wonders of its day. No less a person than President Ulysses S. Grant was among the people who came to marvel at it. And his soul very nearly was saved by the preacher he heard

Oh! To be young again and in love! There is a lot to love on the Vineyard, but to these young people, the best thing is their horses, and showing them at the Dukes County Horse Show.

there that afternoon. According to legend, as the hard-drinking, cigar-smoking former general began to walk forward to renounce his wicked ways, he was gently restrained by his Attorney General, George Williams. It proved once again, depending on your point of view, of course, that it's probably a good idea to have a lawyer at your side when you are faced with life-altering decisions.

It has always been good politics for a president to embrace Christianity, but what Williams must have known was that the Baptists also had a thriving revival encampment at East Chop, separated from the Methodists by Lake Anthony or, as they preferred to describe it, "over Jordan." Eventually both were surrounded by fun-seekers who even had the audacity to patronize one of America's first carousels and gather around the Ocean Park bandstand, where hymns were never on the program. The association that ran the Wesleyan Grove pooled their resources and bought up some of the acreage the promoters were peddling in an effort to hold back the tide, but soon they, too, were bitten by the speculation bug and resold it at a comfortable profit. But their original retreat is still intact, a charming curiosity that serves as a reminder of how souls were saved before television came along.

But there are other ways to refresh your soul than by the fiery words of a revivalist's sermon, and sometimes it almost seems as though that's what God had in mind when He created Martha's Vineyard. It is often summed up in that special feeling you get standing in the Highlands overlooking the Sound, where the tide runs like a millrace but the expanse of green-tinged water has a

Daniel Webster called Gay Head "Niagara Falls without falling water."

Above: a Chilmark barn, enhanced by the Stars and Stripes in its hayloft door.

Where else can you go to jail and still keep smiling except at the Tisbury Street Fair (facing page) in Vineyard Haven?

peaceful stillness in spite of it. The blue sky, accented by billowing white clouds and beams of sunlight reflecting off the water, makes you wish the moment could last for eternity. The breeze brings the smell of salt water with it, but on shore it mixes with the scent of the sweet pepper bush, a delicious odor that will forever afterward bring back memories of that moment and of the Vineyard.

The tall bush with its dotted flowers grows all over the island, but it thrives in the valley around West Tisbury, which seems at first glance to be a farming community that ought to be in the hills of New Hampshire rather than within a short walk from the edge of the sea. The fields are filled with wild grapes and blueberries and you can pick gooseberries by the side of the road. But there is something even more special about West Tisbury. People are usually too busy smelling them to count them, but some say that there isn't a wildflower growing anywhere in Massachusetts that isn't represented in the Vineyard's inland valley. And what nature herself hasn't provided, the residents have found in the seed catalogues that seem to be required reading in West Tisbury over the winter months. It's no coincidence that the Martha's Vineyard Garden Club has its headquarters in the old mill on the pond at the edge of town.

Vineyarders are usually quite

specific when they're giving directions. Everything is either "up-Island" or "down-Island," terms which anywhere else would mean the north and south sides. But not here. Sailors who pilot their ships in an easterly direction are running downward in terms of longitude and vice versa when sailing westward. So on Martha's Vineyard, up is west, not north, and down is east, not south. The imaginary line that separates the two runs between West Tisbury and Edgartown, and the furthest you can walk or ride a bicycle up-Island is the cliffs at Gay Head, which are about as "up" as the Vineyard gets. Gosnold's sailors called the place Dover Cliff because it looked so much like the white cliffs of Dover back home, but the Vineyard's version is more than just chalky white. There are almost as many different colors on the Gay Head cliffs as in the walls of the Grand Canyon, and some Massachusetts chauvinists say their subtlety makes them more beautiful. At 150 feet, Gay Head is hardly in serious competition with the Colorado River's canyon, but Daniel Webster, as enthusiastic a Massachusetts booster as ever lived, once said that it was like Niagara Falls without the falling water. Boosterism notwithstanding, there are few experiences in nature that quite compare to a sunset reflected off the cliffs, especially in late fall when the air is crisp and clear and the sun's angle is low enough to make them seem to glow.

Indian summer, that period of unexpected warmth after the first frost of the fall, is probably the best time of all to be on the Vineyard, and the prevailing southwest wind makes the pleasure last into days when less fortunate New

Oak Bluffs was once aptly named "Cottage City."

Above: summertime at the Campground, Oak Bluffs.

Englanders are rummaging through their trunks to find the earmuffs they discarded back in April. Vineyarders may own snow shovels, but they know they won't have to use them very often and maybe not at all if they have the patience to wait for the salt air to do the job for them. The summer people have long ago gone back home to New York and Boston, and the island's population that reached beyond 75,000 in August is reduced to a more comfortable 14,000 in the winter months. Life goes on at a more leisurely pace and the sea rolls on, a little wilder probably, and the sound of the surf cuts through the crisp air all the way to the center of the island. The ponds freeze and out come the ice skates; someone builds a bonfire and its a toss up whether you'd rather be warming your hands over it or skating out to the center to look up at what must easily be a million stars twinkling over your head.

Soon it will be spring again. You'll feel it in your bones. But the migrating

Above: Edgartown's Glorious Fourth.

birds will announce it, too, and then from the swamps, the tree frogs will begin to sing. They call them pinkletinks on the Vineyard, and their spring song is a call to action. Soon the off-islanders will be back and the cycle of life will change again. But they'll be as welcome as the first warm day in May, because Martha's Vineyard is first and foremost a summer playground, and though there are shore resorts strung up and down the coast from Florida to Maine, none has a welcome mat that compares to the Vineyard's.

Nathaniel Hawthorne once wrote that "For a few summer weeks it is good to live as if the world were heaven." He wasn't thinking of the Vineyard, but he might have been. When the ferry arrives at Edgartown after its five-mile voyage from Wood's Hole, everyone aboard has Hawthorne's words written on their faces.

The Tisbury Street Fair, Vineyard Haven.

Above: the Scottish Bakehouse.

Above: clambake, Oak Bluffs.

Tourism is Martha's Vineyard's only industry these days, and it's what keeps Nantucket alive, too. But the forty-nine-square-mile spot of land thirty miles out at sea, named for the Indian word meaning "faraway island," was one of the most important business centers in early America. When word reached England that trouble was brewing in the colonies, it's very likely that the reports were read by the light of candles made in Nantucket.

But long before Nantucket became a center of world commerce it was well-known as a haven for Quakers. According to legend, Thomas Macy was driven from Salisbury because he had entertained Quakers in his home, and he went with his five children, Edward Starbuck, his neighbor, and a boy named Isaac Coleman to find religious freedom on the island called Nantucket. But whether he consorted with Quakers or not, Macy and his friend Starbuck seem to have been planning the move anyway. Another of their Salisbury neighbors, Tristram Coffin, had already bought the island from Thomas Mayhew for thirty pounds and two beaver hats. Mayhew had acquired the Island along with Martha's Vineyard and the Elizabeth Islands for only forty pounds, so from his point of view it was a good deal. It was a good deal for the Salisburyites, too, and in 1659 eleven families moved to their new homes.

The Quakers didn't come into the picture for nearly fifty years, by which time nearly everybody on Nantucket was related to everyone else in one way or another. They came in the form of

Highjinks in Edgartown.

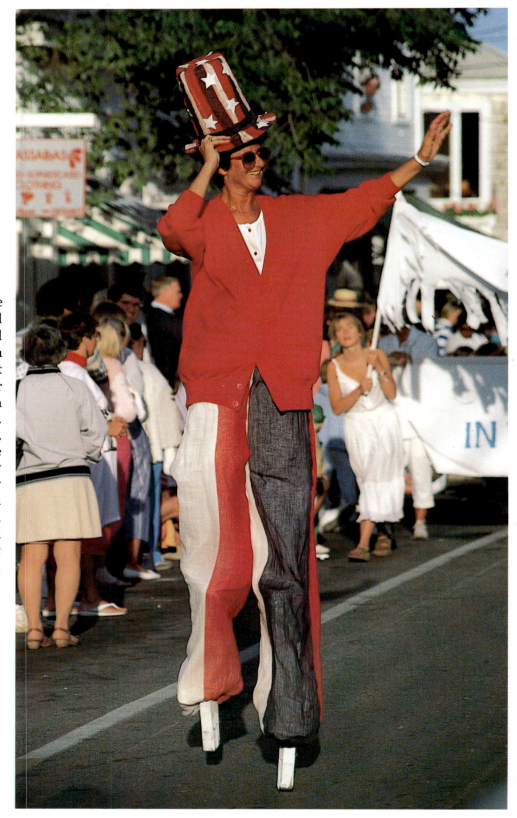

Antique cars are part of the fun at Edgartown's annual Fourth of July Parade. But that's just to crank up your spirits. The fun goes on all day.

missionaries from England who found easy converts in these backsliding Presbyterians and especially in Mary Starbuck, who eventually became one of the most influential preachers of her day. Within twenty years, there were two Quaker meeting houses on the small island and they influenced every aspect of life there right up until the 20th century.

Uncharacteristically, they also controlled the whaling enterprises, a bloody business if ever there was one. But if they were able to turn their backs on the slaughter, they brought integrity to the business side of it and that was one reason why Nantucket dominated the industry for a century and a half. Another was that they were innovators.

In the early days of the Nantucket settlement, Cape Cod farmers had already developed a lucrative sideline in watching for offshore whales and going after them in small boats. It was a hit or miss proposition, and though the so-called "right" whales they went after brought them nice profits there was a better way to real riches. A Nantucket seaman found it in 1712 when a storm blew him out to sea and into the midst of a school of sperm whales. He killed one and when he made his way home, his neighbors got their first glimpse at the future. This was really the right whale to go after. It not only produced more oil, but a waxy substance in its head, known as spermaceti, was a bonus. It not only made better candles, but was valuable as a base for perfume and other cosmetics. The catch was that the creatures were far out in the ocean and it was clear that if an industry was to be created around them some creative effort was called for.

Until then, whales that were killed close to shore were towed to the beach

Squibnocket, one of the Vineyard's private beaches.

where the blubber was melted to a liquid in large fires, a process known as trying-out. After a season or two of inhaling the fumes, which Herman Melville described as smelling "like the left wing on the day of judgement," Nantucketers came up with the idea of installing trying furnaces on the decks of their ships, which not only removed the odors to the open sea, but allowed a ship to collect more whales before heading for home.

The ships they designed for the job were about as unglamorous as any that ever sailed the seas. They were stubby little craft with blunt-nosed bows that made them slow in the water. Rarely more than 125 feet long, they had three short masts that couldn't support enough canvas to produce any burst of speed. But speed wasn't part of the job. Whaling is a classic exercise in patience. Voyages often lasted more than four years but when, often after months of silence, the lookout in one of the crow's nests called out "Thar she blows!" the frenetic activity that followed was incredible.

Every ship had at least five whaleboats aboard, and if the ship itself was an ungainly tub, the boats were masterpieces of seaworthiness. They could ride heavy seas into the teeth of a gale as though they were at rest on a millpond, and they were unbelievably maneuverable, able to turn on a dime even in a heavy wind. When a whale was spotted, the entire crew of thirty, except for the cook and the cooper, who were considered too important to risk their lives, and the cabin boy who was too inexperienced, took to the boats and went out to do battle with the beast.

If they were taking their lives in their hands, there was a better incentive than the thrill of the chase. Everybody

The Charlotte Inn was built in 1820, but it's not Old Hat.

Above: Dukes County Historical Society.

Above: an Edgartown street scene.

Left: Charlotte Inn and the Edgartown Art Gallery.

on board shared the bounty. Depending on his job, each crew member was entitled to a percentage of the oil. After the captain, who was the only man on board to be paid a salary beyond his percentage, the first mate would be entitled to the largest share, which meant that out of the third of the catch reserved for paying the crew, he could claim one barrel of oil for every twenty five on board. The shares decreased down through the ranks, with the cabin boy earning as little as a two hundredth. Typically, a ship collected 2,000 barrels of oil before turning for home, making the crew's share more than 666 barrels. The cabin boy's salary would be three.

It wasn't much, to be sure, but the apprentice was on his way to one day becoming a captain himself, and a walking tour of Nantucket today provides plenty of evidence that it was a job well worth having. By the 1830s, Nantucket, with a population of less than 10,000, was the third richest town in Massachusetts, after Boston and Salem, the home port of the clipper ship fleet. But for all its affluence, Nantucketers couldn't come up with the funds to dredge a channel across the sandbar at the mouth of their harbor. As the whaling ships got larger, so the problem got bigger, and for a few years a floating drydock carried the ships across the bar. But eventually more and more whalers chose to take their cargoes up to New Bedford, and by the turn of the century Nantucket was in a deep decline.

As if to add insult to injury, a great fire swept through the town in 1846. Fueled by the barrels of oil on the docks, it destroyed some 360 buildings. More disastrously it destroyed Nantucket's spirit, and when gold was discovered in

The Edgartown Lighthouse originally marked the harbor at Ipswich, Massachusetts.

Menemsha's fishing fleet brings bass, bluefish, flounder and fat, succulent lobsters, among other great meals, from the waters of Vineyard Sound to the little port of Lobsterville (these pages).

California two years later, she lost a larger percentage of her young people than any other town in Massachusetts. And if any of them had any thoughts of going home again, there were no jobs to go home to because oil recently discovered in the ground was both cheaper and more efficient than whale oil. The whalers still put to sea, but the efficient Confederate Navy blew most of them out of the water and the Civil War gave Nantucket its coup de grace. By 1870, its population had dropped by more than half, and as one of the remaining residents recorded, "... all is silent save the lapping of waves."

Other towns have recovered from similar disasters, but Nantucket's

development stopped right there. It was as if someone had thrown a dustcover over the island and forgotten it was there. But to our generation it was a stroke of luck. Time stood still there for nearly a century, with the result that Nantucket has more authentic examples of 18th- and 19th-century architecture than any other place in America. Even Colonial Williamsburg, which is largely a restoration, has fewer antique buildings than Nantucket. And no amount of historic preservation in other towns will ever produce anything that quite compares with what Nantucket has to offer. If the islanders had tried to pull their town up by the bootstraps, Nantucket would probably have become

Above: celebration at Point Way Inn.

Right: contentment at Charlotte Inn.

a grimy mill town like most of its sister cities over on the mainland. But because they didn't the families who lived there couldn't afford to alter their houses to keep pace with changing architectural fashion. It escaped all the modernizations of the Victorian era and the fads of the early part of this century. Recent building booms have produced their share of boxes with staring windows, but the integrity of the town itself has, mercifully, been spared, and a stroll along its cobblestoned streets shaded by arching elms is almost like walking through a time machine.

Over there at the head of the Square, where it has been standing since 1818, is the Pacific National Bank, a monument to the island's palmier days, when it was the repository for the dollars earned by whales caught in the waters of the South Pacific. It is almost equally important as a testament to the thrifty habits of the Quaker sea captains who rode out the storm of hard times virtually unscathed. Their mansions tell

the story even better. The most spectacular of them are elegant examples of the Greek Revival Style, the first choice for making a statement of affluence in the early 19th century. In most parts of America such mansions are often set well back on manicured lawns, but in Nantucket they are close to the brick sidewalk and most, especially on Main Street, are close together. Available space had little to do with it. Nantucket seems like a quaint, small town today, but what the men who built it had in mind was a great city, and they preferred to plan for privacy by having the garden out back rather than in front. Their closeness was also part of a vague idea of creating a cityscape, but it provided comfort for the seamen's wives who were often alone with their children for years on end.

It wasn't that they didn't have their hands full. In spite of long periods of separation from their husbands, most of them had large families to take care of. And in an age when women were expected to stay home and take care of

the babies, they ran the affairs of the town. With most of the men at sea, they had to, of course, but it's also quite possible that even if the men stayed home, they'd have had to take a back seat to the Nantucket women. They were made of strong stuff. First among them was Mary Coffin, who married Nathaniel Starbuck and became the mother of ten. But she seems to have had what we'd call charisma these days, and when she spoke everyone listened. It was her conversion to Quakerism that put the sect's stamp on the island for two centuries, but her legacy went much deeper. The town's history is full of strong women, including Lucretia Mott, who left the island at an early age, but took some of its traditions with her and became one of the earliest and most influential abolitionists. She was also among the first to make speeches in favor of votes for women. The list also includes Maria Mitchell, whose birthplace is one of New England's most fascinating museums. While she was still a little girl, Maria spent long evenings with her father studying the stars through a telescope. And one night in 1847 she became the first person to see a new comet in the sky. The discovery earned her a gold medal from the King of Denmark and she became the first woman to be offered membership in the Academy of Arts and Sciences. But the woman whaling captains relied on to check the accuracy of their navigational instruments was also a bit of a young Turk. Even before she became a world-recognized scientist and Vassar College's first professor of astronomy, she had renounced Quakerism and, like other Nantucket women, became a champion of women's rights. It was only natural. The equality that American women

The ferry to Chappaquiddick is called "On Time" because it doesn't have a schedule.

Edgartown's Victorian Inn (above) is a Gothic delight in a town noted for its Greek Revival buildings. It remains as true to its distinctive era as they are to theirs.

Edgartown's main business section is short, but sweet. You can spend the whole day there and find perfect memories.

consider newly-earned was a way of life in Nantucket more than a century ago.

In the town's heyday, all the women spent a great deal of their time visiting with each other, but their afternoon tea parties weren't devoted to idle gossip. Such things don't square with Quaker tradition, for one thing, but these women had important matters on their minds. They were the heads of their households in an era when men were expected to be in charge. Many of them had also gone to sea with their husbands and had more than the average woman's global outlook, in spite of a life that could easily have made them insular. But even if some Nantucket women chose to share long voyages to the South Seas, most

stayed home and the houses they lived in usually had a unique feature that showed where their hearts were. It is a balustraded platform on the ridge of the roof that was originally called a "Nantucket walk," but later became known in other places where it was imitated as the "widow's walk," because so many seamen's wives watched from them for ships that never came home. As whaling declined, many of the walks were removed, but enough remain to remind us of the loneliness of life in old Nantucket.

The affluent 19th century is far from the only period represented in Nantucket. The Jethro Coffin house is the oldest, dating back to 1686, but there

The American eagle carries a message that sums up the mood of the Vineyard.

are parts of other houses that are even older. Early Nantucketers tended to move a lot, and when they did they took their old houses with them, adding new elements, usually to make them bigger. Their houses followed the saltbox style prevalent in 17th-century New England, but in Nantucket they called them lean-tos'. Only the name was different. It is a two-story house with its roof sloping down to a single story in back, easy to build, economical to heat and simple to expand. Eventually, they started out larger and expansion came in the form of wings. As fashion changed on the mainland, the islanders followed suit with more stately houses but, thanks to the Quaker tradition of plainness, they were more severe than their counterparts across the water.

Today, they work together to create a special charm, but many visitors think that the seaside cottages at Siasconset, which they are careful to pronounce 'Sconset as the locals do, are quite the most charming structures anywhere in America. They could be right. The little cottages, covered from their foundations to the ridge of their roofs with pink rambling roses and surrounded by stately hollyhocks, are reminders, along with the sign at the end of the road that reads, " To Portugal, 3,000 miles," of the days when Portuguese fishermen established the village and lived on the bluffs overlooking the sea. During the hundred years or so when they were the only people in Siasconset, their homes were more properly described as shanties than cottages and there were no rosebushes, picket fences or window boxes to brighten them up. Such touches came in the early years of the last century, when people who lived in Nantucket Town eight miles away turned the

An iron gray and a dapple gray graze within sight of the sea near Chilmark.

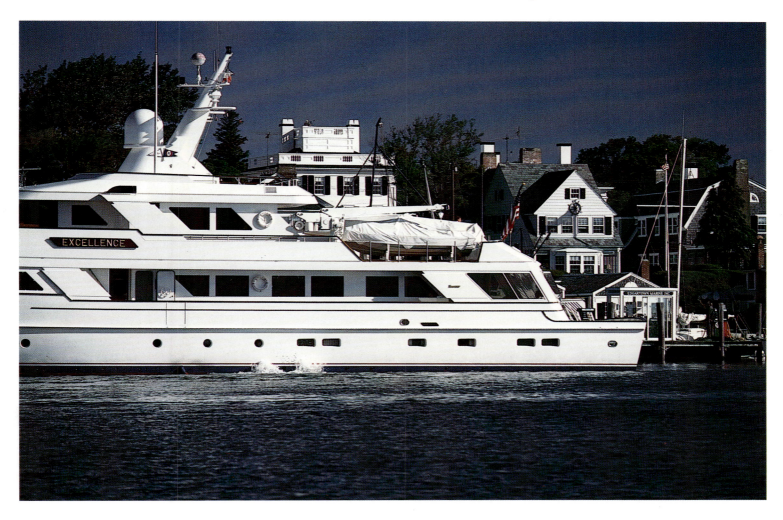

Above: it's not your average houseboat, but the mansions on Edgartown harbor aren't your average houses either.

The Fresnel lens (facing page) that once magnified the light at Gay Head Lighthouse is now in a small tower in the grounds of the Dukes County Historical Society.

fishing village into their own private summer resort. A few of the cottages they built were recycled structures moved out from town, and the general setting wasn't much different from the neighborhoods where they spent the winter. But it was a place to get away from it all, and it was easier to move eight miles over land than thirty over water, even if the road between Nantucket Town and Siasconset was so deeply rutted in the sand that it took three hours to make the trip.

Possibly because of the trip, Nantucketers managed to keep Siasconset a secret until the 1870s, when off-islanders began showing up. The locals were able to keep them from being

too exuberant with their buildings, and though the little tourist boom began expanding the colony, its character didn't change. And that's what attracted the actors. Around 1900, a stage star came to Siasconset, and during his stay he entertained some of his colleagues, who made the village a prime topic of conversation at winter gambols of the Lamb's Club, the actor's fraternity back in New York. The following year, curious Lambs descended on the village, and by 1906 more than fifty of the brightest stars of the theater owned property there, exerting enough influence to change the name of Siasconset's main street to Broadway. Eventually Vaudeville and the movies elbowed the dramatic actors

Above: mermaid and friend.

It's a treat to beat your feet in the Gay Head mud (above).

It's also a treat to use the multicolored mud to create a body beautiful.

aside, and the show business elite began summering in different places—Martha's Vineyard among them – but the legacy of Siasconset's actor's colony is still strong and the village is still a mecca for artists and writers. And almost everyone there is still grumbling that the town fathers decided in 1918 to allow automobiles on its streets.

But anyone who is really serious about Siasconset knows that the best way to enjoy it is on foot. The footpath along the bluffs from the center of town out to Sankaty lighthouse is arguably the pleasantest place to walk on the entire East Coast. The beach, which is known as having the best surf in New England, is quite far out these days, though old-timers say they can remember when it was so close to the town that a strong nor'easter would drive the waves across Broadway. But it's easy to see the ocean from the top of the bluff and to watch the shore birds, the constantly changing sky and the moody colors of the sea itself. It is almost impossible to arrive at Sankaty with a negative thought in your head. And the walk back works even more wonders.

But many strollers prefer to keep on going out onto the moor and up to Altar Rock, at 90 feet one of the island's highest points for a view that on a clear day takes in almost the entire island. To the north across the hills is Nantucket Sound, to the south, the Atlantic Ocean, and across the way, the eight-mile harbor of Nantucket Town itself. Some forty miles off to the southeast, at the limit of the shoals, is where the Nantucket lightship once marked the edge of the ocean highway between New York and Europe.

The view isn't obstructed by trees. Those that grow on Nantucket are kept short by the constant wind from the sea

One of many painters to be seen attempting to match those Gay Head colors on canvas.

and the salt spray that comes with it. But the wind also brings the warming effect of the nearby Gulf Stream, which encourages the growth of some plants that don't normally exist this far north, and the island is the only place in the United States where some varieties of heather grow. There are several varieties out on the moors, a ten-thousand-acre expanse of gently rolling hills covered not only with heather but with indigo, wood lilies, wild roses, bayberry and Scotch broom, huckleberry and beach plum, not to mention the bane of all beaches, poison ivy. There is also a cranberry bog out there, said to be the biggest in the world. In spring and summer, the moors are covered in a blanket of green, but in the fall they are dressed in shades of red and yellow and purple with patches of what looks like pure gold, in a display that is every bit as beautiful as that in the forests of Vermont and New Hampshire, which is where all the visitors to New England have gone in October. And that, of course, is one more reason why Nantucketers think that late fall is the best time to be on their island.

Among the island's year-round residents is a small herd of white-tailed deer, and it is inevitable that at some point during the summer season a first-time visitor will ask how they managed the long swim from the mainland. The answer is that they had help.

Nantucket was dumped out at sea by a melting glacier 8,000 years ago, and there never has been a land bridge to make it possible for any animals to make their way there. Except for mice and shrews, there aren't any four-legged

Nantucket and Martha's Vineyard are only twenty miles apart, but the trip between them can be high adventure when it's a race.

creatures native to the island. The deer arrived in 1922, when a local fisherman found one swimming in the ocean a few miles off Cape Cod. He took pity on the creature, loaded it aboard his boat and took it home to Nantucket. It was a male without a mate, but a summer resident solved its problem of loneliness by bringing two does with him when he arrived a year or two later. It wasn't long before Nantucket had hundreds of deer and a deer hunting season.

It has always been a good place for hunting waterfowl. Or better still, watching them. Nantucket is located along the eastern flyway for migrating birds and is an inviting resting place for them. And hundreds of species make the island their year-round home. Its ponds are a paradise for ducks and geese and herons and its 55 miles of shoreline is home to a host of different kinds of seabirds. But songbirds add to the pleasure, too. There are no thick forests to shelter them, but the food supply is almost without limit.

The tourist business is what keeps food on Nantucket tables these days. The islanders are friendly enough to their summer guests, but even families that have been coming back year after year for generations are not quite accepted as Nantucketers, no matter what their contribution. Among their contributions was the long-delayed dredging of the harbor entrance and the building of jetties to keep the troublesome sandbar from coming back. If they couldn't afford to do the job to save the whaling business, it became apparent at the turn of the century that if ferries loaded with visitors were going to make Nantucket a port of call the work had to be done. But once having made it possible

Victorian splendor is almost an Oak Bluffs trademark.

The shingled buildings (above) in Menemsha seem to have their sleeves rolled up, ready for work. ...

... while the modern structures overlooking the water at Gay Head have the welcome mat out ready for fun.

for the big vessels to use their harbor, Nantucketers felt they had been betrayed when passengers began arriving with those new-fangled automobiles. In the opinion of many locals it was another kick in the pants from the petroleum industry. There wasn't any place on the island you couldn't walk to, they said, and if you didn't like to walk, why, they'd be pleased to get you where you wanted to go with a horse and wagon. Some wagons even had rocking chairs to make the journey pleasanter. And to reinforce their opinions, they made motorcars illegal. But in 1918 they bowed to pressure and began letting them in. By the end of the summer, there were nearly a hundred of them chugging along the sandy roads. The big wheeled dune buggies would come later. So would the mopeds.

But for all that, Nantucket's real rewards are found on foot. The town is often choked with standstill traffic and its cobblestone streets make for a bumpy ride when a car gets moving. But it's a place of pure joy for strolling. Even the plainest of the Quaker houses has little details that can escape the eye when seen through the windshield of a car. And to drive any sort of a vehicle out onto the fragile moors is almost a criminal act. More important, it defeats the purpose of the visit. Motorized, you miss the scents of the heath, the sounds of the birds and the chance to feel the natural rhythm of life that makes Nantucket unique.

Nantucketers say that the best time to go into town during July and August is the middle of a hot afternoon when all their guests are out at the beach. But even at times like that, there are plenty of relatively deserted beaches and it is

The hills of Chilmark.

possible to walk along them for hours in complete solitude. And what a completely marvelous experience it is. The sun is beating down, but the cool wind from the sea counteracts it. And behind you, dunes rise up to shut out the world. Even your own footprints disappear as the waves wash the sand, and you are in a place made new with each breaking wave.

Like most natural forces, the action of the sea is almost imperceptible, but relentless nonetheless. Each wave moves sand in front of it, and the sun dries it so that the wind can carry it further. Soon it will pile up and provide a foundation for seeds carried by birds, and before long grass will appear, its roots anchoring the sand in dunes that will eventually hold back the ocean. They will also protect the land behind them from the constant wind, giving shelter to larger plants like bayberry, beach plums and wild roses, which are not only a delight for eyes and noses, but anchor even more sand and provide even more protection for the island. Among the more beautiful flowers that grow in such places along Nantucket's beaches is the pink and white salt spray rose, which arrived a century ago aboard a ship from the Orient that was wrecked in the treacherous shoals off shore. Once its seeds washed up on the beach, the plants thrived, and the birds have been at work ever since spreading them further inland.

But what the sea gives, it also takes away. The original town on Nantucket was abandoned for its present location because the harbor was closed off by shifting sands, and boaters with last year's chart of Nantucket Sound might be surprised to find themselves aground on a bar that wasn't there a year ago. The

If you like antiques, you'll love the Vineyard.

You can buy almost everything at Alley's General Store (above) in West Tisbury. And if you prefer buying by mail, the Post Office is there, too.

Folks have been meeting on the porch at Edgartown's Harbor View since 1891.

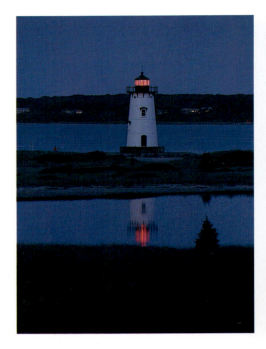

Above: the Edgartown Lighthouse.

ocean is reducing the south shore beach by about eight feet a year, and not long ago Great Point lighthouse at the island's eastern tip crashed into the sea. There had been a tower there since 1784, and the one that was destroyed dated back to 1818 and was built of stone lined with brick. Experts say that Sankaty Light is in danger of the same fate, even though it has defied the sea since 1850. And as if to prove the prediction is true, homeowners on the nearby bluffs are watching their lawns get smaller and smaller each year.

For all the change, though, Nantucket is in no danger of sinking beneath the waves. And in spite of traffic jams and crowds of summer people, she isn't in any danger of losing her charms, either. The grandchildren of today's visitors will still be lured back summer after summer, and the year-rounders will still think of them as "off-islanders." But respectfully, of course.

A musical moment at Oak Bluffs.

Nantucket lives up to its name: "The Little Gray Lady of the Sea."

Gunny Stackpole is the miller-in-residence at Nantucket's Old Mill (these pages), built in 1746 of wood from an old sailing ship. The mill still grinds corn, which is poured through a hole in a revolving stone.

The big oak spindle in the center of the Old Mill (above) reaches up to the horizontal shaft, where it engages with a wheel studded with wooden teeth.

The cast iron structure on Nantucket's Main Street was originally a drinking fountain for horses.

The red roofs of the Coast Guard Station at Brant Point and Steamboat Wharf dominate the entrance to Nantucket Harbor (above).

The sea is getting closer, but Sankaty Head Light (facing page), near Siasconset, has bravely defied it since 1850.

Old North Wharf is a survivor of Nantucket's whaling days.

Above: a reproduction of the figurehead from an old sailing ship, a reminder of the men who financed its voyages.

The oldest house in Siasconset, Auld Lang Syne, has been there since before 1700, when it was a fisherman's hut.

The three identical Georgian mansions on Main Street, Nantucket, known as the "Three Bricks," were built in 1838 by a prosperous whaling merchant, Joseph Starbuck, for his three sons.

For more than fifty years, the Starbuck houses (above) in Nantucket were the social center of this part of Main Street, called the "Court End."

What man creates, nature enhances.

Siasconset was once a summer hideaway for Nantucketers themselves.

Window shopping (left) is an exciting experience in Nantucket, but it's even more stimulating to go inside the shops, where the antiques are not only unique, but dramatically displayed (above).

Carving designs on whale bone and ivory (top and above), the art known as skrimshaw, is part of the Nantucket tradition. But to do it right, you first have to catch a whale. Find out about that at the Whaling Museum (left).

Wonders never cease at Nantucket's Whaling Museum.

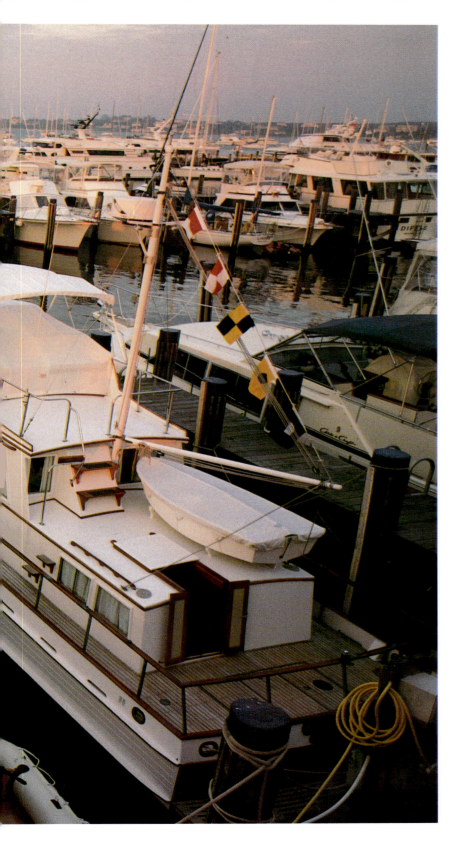

Nantucket's new boat basins, surrounded by three restored wharves, are a continuing boat show all summer long.

Lobster traps are a constant reminder that, for all its pleasure boats, Nantucket is still a working harbor. But then, who ever said there is no pleasure in a lobster dinner?

Day trippers from Hyannis are always welcome on Nantucket.

The men who once tended the lonely Nantucket Lightship passed the hours making baskets (above) that have become a symbol of the island itself.

The lightship baskets are still made carefully by hand, which makes them an expensive souvenir. But you'll never have to buy a replacement.

Brant Point Light (facing page) marks the entrance to Nantucket Harbor.

Time stands still on many Nantucket streets (above), and it is easy to forget that the number of stars in the flag has grown to fifty.

O.K., where should we go on our bike hike? Capetown is a bit far, but look – Sconset is just down the road.

Should you pedal your bike from Nantucket to Wauwinet, the sand will present a challenge, but the flowers along the way make the trip worthwhile.

Sometimes it's easier to push your bike along Nantucket's cobblestones.

Great Point (above), at Nantucket's northernmost corner, is still a long sail from Cape Cod.

The beach at Siasconset is an even longer haul from the next landfall – Portugal.

The Chanticleer in Siasconset, Nantucket, regularly appears on lists of the top fifty restaurants in the world, and its wine list is usually in the world's top ten. The inn was converted to a restaurant by Jean-Charles Berreut, who went to Nantucket as personal chef to one of his countrymen. He fell in love with the place and never went home to France — except to shop for special wines. The Chanty Bar is attached to the restaurant.

Look what you'll miss if you spend Sunday afternoon on the beach.

The Nantucket Moors have been called "The Commons" since the island's earliest days. They are uncommonly beautiful, filled with heather and other plants that scent the air. A horseback ride leads to hidden forests and ponds and cranberry bogs.

The Methodist Church (above) was built in 1823. Its Greek Revival portico was added nearly twenty years later.

The Hadwen House on Main Street is one of a pair once owned by William Hadwen, a silversmith who married a daughter of Joseph Starbuck and began investing in whaling ships. They are among Nantucket's earliest and best examples of Greek Revival architecture.

The Jared Coffin House, now an inn, is an elegant memorial to a descendant of Tristram Coffin, one of the founders of the town.

It's hard to get lost in Nantucket, but if you get confused, the signs (above) will help you find your way.

The last roses of summer bring sadness to visitors, but Nantucketers know the best is yet to come.

The only thing that can improve a bowl of Nantucket clam chowder is a salad to go with it. Get that at the farmer's market (facing page).

Pushing the boat out in downtown Nantucket.

What's more fun than shopping? Shopping in Nantucket, of course.

Above: a lifeguard.

The blues are running – a surf caster's dream comes true.

Boating may be great fun, but it doesn't compare to tying up at the Nantucket boat basins.

Above: a precarious perch, but the catch of the day makes it all worthwhile.

Black-backed and herring gulls share beach space, but they can get quite vocal on the subject of sharing food.

Painting on the beach at Wauwinet.

How fresh is the fish you buy on Nantucket? It's so fresh you may have to wait for the boat to dock before you pick it up.

The sign hasn't been hanging there since 1784, but it might have been. There had been a settlement on Nantucket for a century and a quarter by then.